CULTURAL CONTRIBUTIONS FROM

EUROPE

THE PRINTING PRESS, BRAILLE, AND MORE

GREAT CULTURES,
GREAT IDEAS

MADELINE TYLER

PowerKiDS
press

Published in 2019 by The Rosen Publishing Group, Inc.
29 East 21st Street, New York, NY 10010

Cataloging-in-Publication Data

Names: Tyler, Madeline.
Title: Cultural contributions from Europe: the printing press, braille, and more / Madeline Tyler.
Description: New York : PowerKids Press, 2019. | Series: Great cultures, great ideas | Includes glossary and index.
Identifiers: LCCN ISBN 9781538338223 (pbk.) | ISBN 9781538338216 (library bound) | ISBN 9781538338230 (6 pack)
Subjects: LCSH: Europe--Juvenile literature.| Europe--Intellectual life--Juvenile literature. |
Europe--Civilization--Juvenile literature. | Europe--Social life and customs--Juvenile literature. | Civilization--European influences.
Classification: LCC D1051.T954 2019 | DDC 940--dc23

Written by: Madeline Tyler
Edited by: Kirsty Holmes
Designed by: Gareth Liddington

Photo credits
Abbreviations: l-left, r-right, b-bottom, t-top, c-center, m-middle.

Front Cover – siraphat, FPWing, koosen, Sergiy1975, Tania Zbrodko, mrwood, Katia Karpel, Evgeny Karandaev, 2 - Andrey Prokhorov, 4 - stocker1970, Jakkarin Apikornrat, Creative-Touch, AJP, Sirisak Chantorn, Memory Stockphoto, piyaphong, 5 - AJ Frames, DisobeyAr, Sata Production, Jennifer Lam, Kamil Macniak, 6 - Magdanatka, I am Corona, hxduyl, 7 - sebasnoo, Heath Doman, Maximumvector, charnsitr, 8 - vivat, 3RUS, dimbar76, 10 - S-F, catwalker, 11 - JurateBuiviene, Roman Yanushevsky, 12 - MIGUEL GARCIA SAAVEDRA, Capitolo dei Domenicani, Africa Studio, 13 - Allexxandar, irynal, 14 - J. A. V. Turck, Anneka, 15 - spr, Osugi, KOKTARO, 16 - vectorfusionart, Snowman 2016, 17 - Pavel Ignatov, chombosan, 18 - gallofoto, tommaso lizzul, 19 - Rawpixel.com, Freedom_Studio, 20 - Nationaal Archief, Vadim Sadovski, 21 - Romjia, JPagetRFPhotos, 22 - Natali Li, padu_foto, Martynova Anna, 23 - ruigsantos, kanvag, 24 - Photobac, Bobo Ling, 25 - Emily Marie Wilson, George Grantham Bain, 26 - Danny Smythe, Khosro, 27 - Byelikova Oksana, 28 - ESOlex, Vladimir Volodin, Vankherson, 29 - Alexanderphoto7, Mariia Masich, 30 - ricochet64, nomadFra, byggarn.se.

Images are courtesy of Shutterstock.com. With thanks to Getty Images, Thinkstock Photo and iStockphoto.

All facts, statistics, web addresses and URLs in this book were verified as valid and accurate at time of writing. No responsibility for any changes to external websites or references can be accepted by either the author or publisher.

Manufactured in the United States of America

CPSIA Compliance Information: Batch #CSPK18: For Further Information contact Rosen Publishing, New York, New York at 1-800-237-9932.

CONTENTS

Words that look like **this**
are explained in the glossary on page 31.

WHAT IS CULTURE?

If you were to travel around the world, visiting lots of countries on the way, you would probably notice that certain things around you would not be the same as they are at home. The countries and places you visit, and the people you meet, would have different languages, customs, and ways of doing things. The food might be different, the way people dress might be different, and even the laws and rules might be different to what you know at home. All of these things, when put together, make up what we call the culture of a place.

A HOUSE IN CHINA MIGHT LOOK VERY DIFFERENT THAN ONE IN THE UK!

WHAT MAKES UP A CULTURE?

Shared ideas and traditions that make up a culture can include:

LAWS	HOLIDAYS
FOOD	FAMILIES
LEADERS	SCHOOLS
SYMBOLS	SPECIAL BUILDINGS
BELIEFS	HOSPITALS
CEREMONIES	ENTERTAINMENT

A culture can also be shared by a group of people who might not live near each other, but who share a way of life. People who like the same music or hobbies can share a culture.

People who all belong to the same religion can be said to share a culture, no matter where they live.

BEAUTIFUL HENNA TATTOOS ARE PART OF INDIAN CULTURE. MANY INDIAN BRIDES AROUND THE WORLD PRACTICE THIS CULTURAL TRADITION.

Our culture is a big part of our identity. Having a distinctive culture is what makes places or people unique. Knowing you belong to a particular culture is a good feeling. It's nice to share our culture with other people. If we are in a culture we recognize, we understand what to do or how to act.

DIFFERENT CULTURES GREET EACH OTHER IN DIFFERENT WAYS – A HANDSHAKE, A BOW, OR EVEN A KISS!

GLOBAL CULTURE

Even though every culture is different and has many things that make it unique, many cultures also have lots of things in common. We can learn a lot from other cultures, and share the things we know and like. In the past, when people started traveling and visiting other cultures, they began to swap and share their food, traditions, and knowledge, and people started to adopt things from other cultures into their own. For example, British people see drinking tea as part of their cultural identity – but tea is originally from China and is also an important part of Japanese culture.

AFTERNOON TEA, WITH CAKES AND SANDWICHES, IS A TRADITIONAL PART OF ENGLISH CULTURE.

IN JAPAN, THE TEA CEREMONY IS AN IMPORTANT CULTURAL RITUAL.

It is also really interesting to explore other cultures and discover new and exciting ways of doing things! We can share our ideas and learn new things when cultures meet.

TEA WAS ORIGINALLY FROM CHINA AND ORIGINATED DURING THE SHANG DYNASTY.

MY CULTURE, YOUR CULTURE, OUR CULTURE

Adopting ideas from other cultures can lead to really interesting results. Many cultures take inspiration from others and adapt and change their traditions and customs to make them their own. Putting two ideas from two different cultures together can produce new and exciting things. Did you know that a pizza in Italy will look very different from a pizza in the US? Italians introduced pizza, a traditional Italian dish, to the Americans living in the US. A traditional Italian pizza has a thin, crispy crust, and lots of tomato, but only a small amount of mozzarella cheese. An American pizza has a thick, fluffy base, is smothered in cheese, and can have lots of different toppings – meats, fish, even pineapple! Both cultures share a love for pizza, but each culture has their own way of doing things!

TRADITIONAL ITALIAN PIZZA

WHICH PIZZA DO YOU PREFER? ITALIAN, AMERICAN, OR MAYBE A SLICE OF EACH?

DEEP DISH AMERICAN PIZZA

WHERE IS EUROPE?

Europe is the second smallest **continent** in the world and is made up of 50 countries. Europe can be found in both the Eastern and the Northern **hemispheres**.

CAN YOU SPOT WHERE EUROPE IS?

England

Capital City: London
Population: 54,800,000 people
Size: 50,302 square miles (130,282 sq km)
Currency: Pounds sterling
Major religions(s): Christianity (Church of England)
Main language(s): English

Germany

Capital city: Berlin
Population: 82,100,000 people
Size: 137,879 square miles (357,105 sq km)
Currency: Euro
Major religion(s): Christianity
Main language(s): German

France

Capital city: Paris
Population: 65,000,000 people
Size: 210,026 square miles (543,965 sq km)
Currency: Euro
Major religion(s): Christianity (Catholicism)
Main language(s): French

Spain

Capital city: Madrid
Population: 46,400,000 people
Size: 195,364 square miles (505,990 sq km)
Currency: Euro
Major religion(s): Christianity (Catholicism)
Main language(s): Castilian Spanish, Catalan, Valencian, Galician, Basque

MADRID, SPAIN

The Netherlands

Capital city: Amsterdam
Population: 17,000,000 people
Size: 16,158 square miles
(41,849 sq km)
Currency: Euro
Major religion(s): Christianity
Main language(s): Dutch

Sweden

Capital city: Stockholm
Population: 9,900,000 people
Size: 172,756 square miles
(447,435 sq km)
Currency: Krona
Major religion(s): Christianity
Main language(s): Swedish

Romania

Capital city: Bucharest
Population: 19,600,000 people
Size: 92,046 square miles
(238,398 sq km)
Currency: New leu
Major religion(s): Christianity
Main language(s): Romanian

Russia

Capital city: Moscow
Population: 144,000,000 people
Size: 6,602,000 square miles
(17,099,101 sq km)
Currency: Russian ruble
Major religion(s): Orthodox
Christianity
Main language(s): Russian

Italy

Capital city: Rome
Population: 54,400,000 people
Size: 116,347 square miles
(301,337 sq km)
Currency: Euro
Major religion(s): Christianity
(Catholicism)
Main language(s): Italian

VATICAN CITY

Vatican City is an **independent state** in Rome, the capital of Italy. It is the smallest independent state in the world and has been the main home of the **Catholic Church** for around 1,700 years.

Although Vatican City was officially made a state in 1929, it has been a **pilgrimage** site for Catholic followers for hundreds of years. Vatican City now receives more than 5 million visitors every year—some visit as a religious pilgrimage, while others travel to Vatican City to admire the museums and artwork there.

VATICAN CITY IS FOUND WITHIN ROME.

THESE ARE SOME EXAMPLES OF COINS MADE IN VATICAN CITY. THEY ARE VERY POPULAR WITH COLLECTORS!

Only around 800 people live in Vatican City, but it has its own banking and telephone systems, post office, newspaper, and radio and television stations. It even makes its own coins and produces its own stamps! Coins from Vatican City are part of the Euro currency and can be used across Italy and other European countries that use the Euro.

ST. PETER'S BASILICA AND THE SISTINE CHAPEL

Vatican City is home to lots of interesting buildings. St. Peter's **Basilica** is a very large church in Vatican City that took 109 years to build—it was started in 1506 but was not completed until 1615! The dome at the top of the basilica was designed by the artist Michelangelo. It took 43 years to complete. It is 466 feet (136 m) high and has been used as a model for many other domes. Some of these include the Saint Paul's Cathedral dome in London and the Capitol Building in Washington, D.C.

ST. PETER'S BASILICA USED TO BE THE LARGEST CHRISTIAN CHURCH IN THE WORLD. TODAY, THE LARGEST CHURCH IS YAMOUSSOUKRO BASILICA IN COTE D'IVOIRE, WHICH WAS BUILT IN 1989.

YAMOUSSOUKRO BASILICA, COTE D'IVOIRE

The Sistine Chapel was built in the Vatican Palace in the 15th century. One of the most famous parts of the Sistine Chapel is its ceiling, which is decorated with **frescoes** painted by Michelangelo at the beginning of the 16th century.

GLASSES

It is difficult to know when and where eyeglasses were invented, but the first country in Europe to begin using them was Italy in the 14th century. Many people believe that eyeglasses were invented by Alessandro di Spina in either Pisa or Florence.

These early glasses were only useful for farsightedness. If you are farsighted, you can see things that are far away, but things that are close will look out of focus and blurry. These glasses were mostly used as reading glasses.

THE FIRST PORTRAIT WITH EYEGLASSES IN IT IS A PAINTING BY TOMMASO DA MODENA. THE PAINTING IS OF HUGH OF SAINT-CHER AND WAS PAINTED IN 1352.

EARLY EYEGLASSES, OR SPECTACLES, WOULD HAVE LOOKED LIKE THESE.

Glasses have changed a lot since the 14th century. They look very different, and can now be worn to correct both farsightedness and **nearsightedness**.

Glasses are worn by young people and old people. Do you know anyone who wears glasses?

TELESCOPE

Have you ever looked up into the night sky and wished you could see the stars and the planets more closely? This is how the idea for the telescope came about. Hans Lippershey was born in the **United Netherlands** in 1570 and worked as a spectacle maker. Many people believe Lippershey was the first person to think about creating a telescope, and he soon drew up some very early designs. The government in the United Netherlands was impressed and paid Lippershey a lot of money for the drawings.

GALILEO
GALILEI

THE LARGEST TELESCOPE IN THE WORLD IS THE GRAN TELESCOPIO DE CANARIAS ON THE ISLAND OF LA PALMA.

Soon, an Italian man called Galileo heard of this idea and created his own telescope. Galileo was the first person to use a telescope to look up at the sky. He discovered four of Jupiter's moons and even saw craters on the Moon! Telescopes were an amazing invention that allowed scientists and astronomers to discover new planets and stars.

CALCULATORS

Math can be quite tricky, and sometimes it is faster to do sums on a calculator than in your head. Can you imagine trying to work out 6,894,035 x 7,098 without a calculator? Hundreds of years ago, before calculators were invented, people had to!

Gottfried Wilhelm von Leibniz was a German mathematician. Leibniz built on the French mathematician Blaise Pascal's ideas. Some years later, he created the first ever mechanical calculator that could add, subtract, divide, and multiply. His invention was called a "step reckoner."

THIS IS WHAT LEIBNIZ'S "STEP RECKONER" LOOKED LIKE. IMAGINE TRYING TO CARRY THIS TO SCHOOL!

01001000 01101001 00100001

Those numbers are not random – they are binary code! As well as creating the "step reckoner," Leibniz also developed the binary code. Leibniz came up with the idea to use just two digits in the code: 0 and 1. This could easily be understood by computers and is still used today!

NOW WE USE ELECTRONIC CALCULATORS INSTEAD OF MECHANICAL CALCULATORS.

PRINTING PRESS

Although some types of printing, involving wooden blocks and movable stamps, already existed in China, Germany was the first country to invent mechanized printing. In the 15th century, Johannes Gutenberg invented a machine called the "printing press." Even though the printing press was powered by hand, it could still print 250 sheets of printed paper per hour. Printing methods before this could only produce around 50 pages a day!

THE FIRST BOOK THAT WAS PRINTED BY THE GUTENBERG PRESS WAS THE GUTENBERG BIBLE. 200 COPIES WERE PRINTED, AND AROUND 50 STILL EXIST TODAY.

INKJET PRINTING

The Gutenberg press allowed books to be printed very quickly. This made books a lot cheaper and meant that they could be spread easily across Europe. Libraries soon grew, and people could learn about lots of different topics. Nowadays, **inkjet printing** and **laser printing** are popular methods, but the wooden printing press developed by Gutenberg was used for more than 300 years.

BRAILLE

Two hundred years ago in France, a young boy called Louis Braille had an accident and hurt his eye. Unfortunately, an infection spread to both of Louis's eyes and he became blind. Louis Braille could no longer see, so he came up with an idea to allow blind people to read and write.

While he was a student at the National Institute for Blind Children in Paris, he created a system of dots that could be used to represent letters in the French alphabet. This system is now called "braille."

SOME CHILDREN LEARN TO READ BRAILLE IN SCHOOL.

BRAILLE ALPHABET

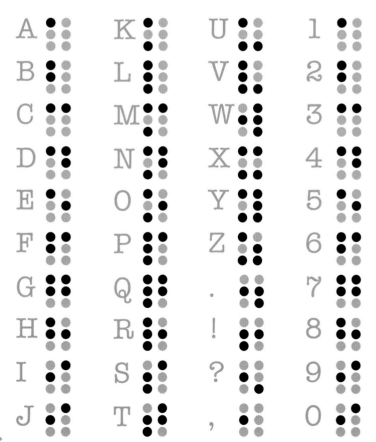

The original braille system was made up of 63 dot patterns. These dot patterns were made within a six-dot cell and each pattern represented a different letter, number or symbol. People can read braille by feeling the raised dots with their fingers. Louis Braille's school began using his system in 1854, and Standard English Braille was created in 1932.

WORLD WIDE WEB

Have you ever wondered what the "www" means at the beginning of a website address? It stands for World Wide Web and was invented by an Englishman called Sir Timothy Berners-Lee.

Berners-Lee developed three technologies, called HTML, URL, and HTTP. These are like special languages for computers, and allow all computers to communicate and understand each other. The World Wide Web is a collection of webpages that can be shared between computers using HTML, URL, and HTTP.

THE WORLD WIDE WEB CAN BE ACCESSED FROM COMPUTERS, TABLETS, SMARTPHONES, AND LAPTOPS.

Berners-Lee's invention meant that everyone could use the Internet, not just scientists. Information could now be shared quickly across the world, and people could contact their friends and family in other countries. There are now almost 4 billion Internet users in the world because of Timothy Berners-Lee's invention.

TELEPHONE

Telephones are useful for contacting people who are far away from us. One of the first telephones was invented by Alexander Graham Bell, from Scotland, at the end of the 19th century. It was very different than the telephones we use today.

THE FIRST TELEPHONE CALL WAS BETWEEN ALEXANDER GRAHAM BELL AND HIS ASSISTANT, THOMAS WATSON. BELL SAID TO WATSON: "MR. WATSON - COME HERE - I WANT TO SEE YOU."

Alexander Graham Bell's mother was **deaf**, and his father taught deaf people how to speak clearly. Eventually, Bell began teaching at the Boston School for Deaf Mutes where he carried out research on the human voice, sound, and sound waves.

Bell's experiments into the science of sound soon led to attempts to send the human voice using an **electric current**. The telephone was born!

MAKE YOUR OWN STRING TELEPHONE!

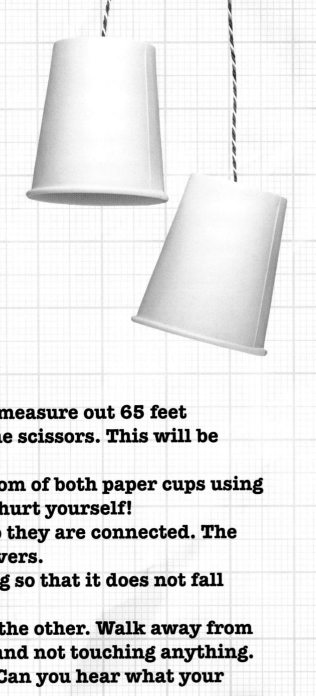

YOU WILL NEED

- **Two paper cups**
- **A sharp pencil**
- **String**
- **Scissors**
- **Ruler or tape measure**

METHOD

1. Using your tape measure or ruler, measure out 65 feet (20 m) of string and cut it using the scissors. This will be your telephone cord.
2. Poke a small hole through the bottom of both paper cups using the sharp pencil. Be careful not to hurt yourself!
3. Pull the string through each cup so they are connected. The cups are now your telephone receivers.
4. Tie a knot at both ends of the string so that it does not fall through the hole.
5. Grab one cup and give your friend the other. Walk away from each other until the string is taut and not touching anything.
6. Take turns speaking into the cup. Can you hear what your friend is saying?

When you speak into a paper cup, the sound turns into vibrations, which travel along the string until they reach the other paper cup. Then the vibrations become sound again, so your friend can hear what you said!

SPACESUITS

When astronauts go up to space, it is important that their spacesuits are pressurized. Air has weight, and down on Earth where there is lots of air in the sky above us, the air pressure is high. However, up in space where there is not much air, the air pressure is low. Low air pressure can be dangerous for humans, so it is important to wear a special suit to protect the body.

OVER 500 HUMANS HAVE BEEN UP TO SPACE, AS WELL AS LOTS OF OTHER ANIMALS INCLUDING MONKEYS, DOGS, AND RABBITS!

EMILIO HERRERA LINARES'S SPACESUIT

During the 1930s, many people were thinking about space, flying, and the protective clothing that would need to be worn. One of the first people to build a **full-pressure suit** was Emilio Herrera Linares in Spain. Herrera created his suit for a 1936 balloon flight up to the **stratosphere**. Unfortunately, because the Spanish Civil War started in 1936, Herrera never got to test his suit in the stratosphere. However, it could be seen as a very early version of the spacesuits that astronauts use today.

FLAMENCO

Flamenco is a type of song, dance, and music most common in Andalusia, in southern Spain. It involves a singer who plays the guitar and sets the rhythm, while someone performs the dance.

Flamenco songs are traditionally very emotional and are usually about death, pain, and sadness. Flamenco is popular throughout Spain during festivals and celebrations.

Although flamenco is an important part of Spanish culture and is now considered a Spanish dance, it was produced from mixing lots of different cultures. When some people in India **migrated** to Spain between the 9th and 14th centuries, they brought bells, tambourines, castanets, and many different songs and dances. Flamenco was born out of the combination of this traditional music with the cultures of the Spanish **Jews** and **Moors**.

PEOPLE OF ALL AGES CAN ENJOY FLAMENCO.

TETRIS

Tetris is a video game that was created by Alexey Pajitnov in 1984. The idea of the game is to rotate shapes that fall from the top of the screen. The shapes fit together to create solid lines which then disappear.

Tetris was very popular on Nintendo Game Boy and is now available on most video game consoles and computers.

In 2014, game designer Frank Lee broke the Guinness World Record for largest display of a video game on a building. Two players controlled a game of Tetris using joysticks, which was projected onto two sides of a 29-story skyscraper over 1 mile (1.6 km) away! The smallest game of Tetris was played in Amsterdam using a microscope. Scientists played it using very tiny pieces of microscopic glass.

MATRYOSHKA DOLLS

Matryoshka dolls have been a popular Russian **souvenir** for around 100 years. The first matryoshka dolls were carved in 1892 and represented **peasant** life. The dolls carried a chicken, a basket, a **sickle**, a bowl of porridge, and a broom.

Matryoshka dolls are sometimes called nesting dolls because they nest inside one another. The largest doll is usually a mother, and the smaller dolls are her children. The dolls symbolize hope for future **generations**.

THE WORD "MATRYOSHKA" IS TAKEN FROM THE RUSSIAN NAME, MATRYONA OR MATRIOSHA. IT IS ALSO SIMILAR TO THE LATIN WORD "MATER," WHICH MEANS MOTHER.

By the early 20th century, matryoshka dolls had become very popular with people from around the world. Now, matryoshka dolls can come in all sorts of designs. Although they used to be painted in traditional Russian clothing, some matryoshka dolls are now decorated as animals or even as famous people.

RUSSIAN BALLET

Ballet is a type of dance that first appeared during the 15th and 16th centuries in Italy and France. Ballet was very popular until the beginning of the 20th century, when people in France began to lose interest and stopped going to see the performances.

When a Russian ballet group called the Ballets Russes arrived in Paris in 1909, people in the rest of Europe began to appreciate ballet again. It was seen as a very special and important type of art.

A STATUE OF THE RUSSIAN BALLERINA, ANNA PAVLOVA, ON TOP OF THE VICTORIA PALACE THEATRE IN LONDON, UK

The Ballets Russes toured around Europe and had a great influence on European ballet. Anna Pavlova, a Russian ballerina, traveled around the world and brought ballet to many people for the first time.

After seeing the Ballets Russes and ballerinas like Anna Pavlova, ballet companies soon began appearing in France, the UK, and the US. Russian ballets are still popular around the world today.

BRAN CASTLE

Have you ever heard of Dracula? He is a **fictional** character who lived in a grand castle in Transylvania. Transylvania is now in Romania, and many people believe that Dracula's castle is actually Bran Castle, in the **Transylvanian Alps** of Romania.

AFTER SHE DIED, QUEEN MARIE'S HEART WAS KEPT AT BRAN CASTLE FOR MANY YEARS.

Bran Castle was built in 1388. Many soldiers lived at the castle and it acted as a **fortress** to protect Transylvania from the **Ottoman Empire**. From 1920 to 1957, it was used as a royal castle by Queen Marie, the queen of Romania. Bran Castle soon became Queen Marie's favorite place to stay.

Now, however, Bran Castle is a museum that tourists can visit to learn about the history of Transylvania and Romania.

VIKINGS

Scandinavia is a region in northern Europe that includes Norway, Sweden, and Denmark. A lot of Scandinavia is in the **Arctic Circle** which makes the **climate** very cold.

Many years ago, towards the end of the 8th century, the inhabitants of Scandinavia sailed in their longboats to the United Kingdom to attack the towns and cities, and invade the land. These invaders were called Vikings. They were **seafaring** warriors, and conquered much of the United Kingdom.

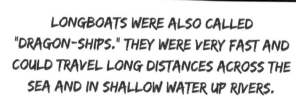

LONGBOATS WERE ALSO CALLED "DRAGON-SHIPS." THEY WERE VERY FAST AND COULD TRAVEL LONG DISTANCES ACROSS THE SEA AND IN SHALLOW WATER UP RIVERS.

The Vikings settled in areas in the north and east of England, the west coast of Scotland, and small parts of Wales and the Republic of Ireland. The Vikings made use of the good farmland in the UK and were able to grow crops and keep animals. The climate in the United Kingdom is a lot warmer than Scandinavia and was better suited for farming.

TALK LIKE A VIKING!

When the Vikings invaded the United Kingdom and settled there, they brought their language to the **Anglo-Saxons**. The Viking invasions ended around 1,000 years ago. However, there are still plenty of reminders of the Vikings in the English language. Can you match the English word with the Old Norse word it came from?

Reindeer	Vindauga
Anger	Renna
Race	Fótr
Run	Angr
Window	Hreindyri
Freckles	Lauss
Foot	Rás
Happy	Skrap
Loose	Gefa
Choose	Happ
Scare	Baggin
Ill	Taka
Bag	Skirra
Scrap	Kjósa
Take	Illr
Give	Freknur

THE WORD 'THURSDAY' COMES FROM THE VIKINGS! IT IS TAKEN FROM THE OLD NORSE WORD "þunresdæg" – THOR'S DAY! IN NORSE MYTHOLOGY, THOR IS THE GOD OF THUNDER.

Answers: Reindeer = Hreindyri, Anger = Angr, Race = Rás, Run = Renna, Window = Vindauga, Freckles = Freknur, Foot = Fótr, Happy = Happ, Loose = Lauss, Choose = Kjósa, Scare = Skirra, Ill = Illr, Bag = Baggin, Scrap = Skrap, Take = Taka, Give = Gefa.

LEGO

Have you ever built something with LEGO bricks? Or maybe played a LEGO game on a gaming console? LEGO is over 70 years old and started as a small company in Denmark, making wooden toys. Now LEGO is best known for its small, colorful plastic bricks that fit together to build different LEGO creations. The first LEGO brick was made a long time ago in 1958, and LEGO still looks the same now. LEGO can be used to make towers, cars, rockets... anything you can imagine!

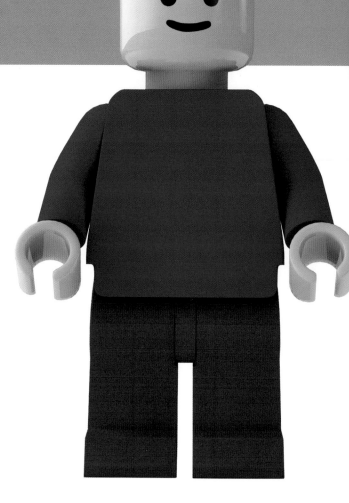

LEGO is so popular that it now makes more than just bricks and **construction** sets. It is now possible to play LEGO-based video games, and in 2014, LEGO released their own movie.

AROUND 20 BILLION LEGO BRICKS ARE MADE EVERY YEAR! THAT IS AROUND 2 MILLION LEGO BRICKS AN HOUR!

LEGOLAND

LEGOLAND is a theme park dedicated to LEGO. There are LEGOLAND resorts in Denmark, Germany, the UK, the United Arab Emirates, Japan, Malaysia, and the US. The rides and attractions are all LEGO-themed, and many of the sculptures in the park are even made out of LEGO!

MOUNT RUSHMORE, LEGOLAND BILLUND

LEGOLAND BILLUND IS BUILT WITH OVER 65 MILLION LEGO BRICKS!

The first LEGOLAND was built in 1968, near the original LEGO factory in Billund, Denmark. As well as roller coasters, LEGOLAND also has many well-known landmarks created out of LEGO. These are miniature sculptures that can be found in a section of the park called Miniland.

There are miniature versions of famous American landmarks like the Statue of Liberty, the Capitol Building, and Mount Rushmore. There are also models of the Taj Mahal (a beautiful **mausoleum** in India) and the Forbidden City (a famous site in China).

IKEA

Did you know IKEA first started in Sweden? IKEA is now a very popular furniture shop that can be found in 51 countries all over the world, but it was not always such a big company. IKEA started with a 5-year-old Swedish boy called Ingvar Kamprad. Ingvar started his business by buying matches cheaply in **bulk** and selling them to his neighbors for a **profit**. Soon, Ingvar was selling flower seeds, greeting cards, and stationery. This was the very beginning of IKEA, but it was not a proper company yet and did not have a name.

THE IKEA WEBSITE RECEIVES AROUND 2.1 BILLION VISITS EVERY YEAR!

THE IKEA LOGO USES THE COLORS OF THE SWEDISH FLAG.

Ingvar started IKEA in 1943, and they originally only sold pens, wallets, picture frames, watches, and jewelry. A few years later, they began selling furniture from catalogs, and now a person can buy a whole kitchen or bathroom from IKEA.

IKEA STORES RECEIVE AROUND 915 MILLION VISITS EVERY YEAR!

GLOSSARY

Anglo-Saxons   people that lived in England when the Vikings invaded

Arctic Circle   the most northerly area on Earth that surrounds the North Pole

basilica   an important Catholic church

bulk   a large amount of something

Catholic Church   a group of Christians who are led by the pope

climate   the common weather in a certain place

construction   building and creating

continent   a very large area of land made up of many countries

deaf   when a person cannot hear well, or at all

electric current   the flow of electricity

fictional   something that is made up and not real

fortress   a large building, like a castle, that is well-protected

frescoes   paintings found on walls and ceilings, common in Italy

full-pressure suit   suits designed to be worn by astronauts in space, where there is very low air pressure

generations   groups of people from the same family or society who are roughly the same age

hemispheres   sections of the Earth, either Northern, Southern, Eastern, or Western

independent state   an area, like a city, that has power over itself and is not under the control of the country it is in

inkjet printing   a type of printing that uses tiny sprays of ink to draw on the paper

Jews   followers of the Jewish religion, Judaism

laser printing   a type of printing that uses a laser beam to transfer images and text onto paper

mausoleum   a large building that holds a tomb inside

migrated   moved from one place to live in a new place

Moors   Muslims that used to live in North Africa and conquered Spain in the 8th century

nearsightedness   the opposite of farsightedness. A person can see things that are close, but things that are far away will look out of focus and blurry

Ottoman Empire   a group that ruled over much of the Middle East and Eastern Europe for over 600 years, starting in 1299

peasant   poor land worker who belonged to the lowest social class

pilgrimage   a religious journey or trek, usually to a specific place or building

profit   earning more money than you originally spent

seafaring   working at sea and confident traveling by sea

sickle   a tool with a curved blade and a short handle, traditionally used to cut long grass and crops

souvenir   items that are bought on vacation in order to remember a place

stratosphere   a layer of the atmosphere, around 30 miles (48 km) above Earth

taut   tightly pulled so that it is not loose

Transylvanian Alps   a group of mountains in Romania

United Netherlands   the Seventeen Provinces of the United Netherlands was formed in 1482 and became Netherlands, Belgium, and Luxembourg in 1581

INDEX

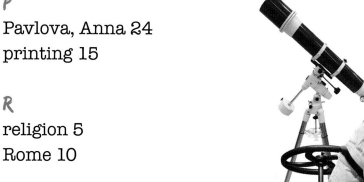
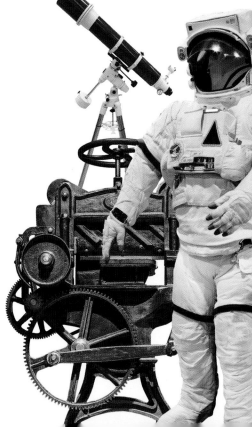